OPEN 24 HOURS

OPEN 24 HOURS

poems

SUZANNE LUMMIS

LYNX HOUSE PRESS
Spokane, Washington

Cover Photo by Marcin Wichary.
Book Design: Christine Holbert.

FIRST EDITION

Cataloging-in-Publication Data is available from the Library of Congress.

ISBN 978-089924-138-8

for Chuck Gresham

CONTENTS

I
Substandard Housing

II
Broken and in Need of Repair

III

The Fate Cookies

I

SUBSTANDARD HOUSING

HOT PURSUIT

It wasn't the grind of brakes, cry
of metals un-forgiving each other—no.
It was that delirious and slow plowing
headlong into and past *Traffic Light,*
Street Lamp, then the disruption
of *Parked Truck,* that got me out of bed
and down four flights of stairs onto
the street. The rubble of smashed
glass makes the sidewalk shine. The traffic
light's lying knocked flat. One

cop car stopped behind the spot,
the other's in pursuit—the kid hit
the ground and took off. By foot.
Everyone's drained out of the Donut Shop,
the Armenian dance hall, Owl Drugs—
homeboys in T-shirts and blue tattoos.
In L.A. it gets like this at night—

hot. We stare at the parked truck
that got punched from the back, then
at the criminal car. Under the flung hood
the motor stamps and steams. Look
at that bumper, we yell, that twisted wheel!
And the glove compartment's sprung, so
the deeds of legal ownership drift

out the driver side. The driver door's
bent wild. It's, like, so ajar. It's like
Chamberlain's sculptures from crushed cars.

Here is the art of disaster, the art
of the split-second fatal bad choice.
I know how our mistakes change
the shape of things but to look
at the twists and turns the kid put
in this Ford coupe you'd think
what he wanted really was to make

a crazy staircase and climb up.

RED SHOES

"I tried on nine pairs," she starts out
in this elevator initialed by renters
who pass each other in halls, on flights
of stairs, then finally must meet,
"and none of them fit." We slide up.
She counts down, "Seven, six-and-a-half,
six, narrow, wide . . ." "I love red shoes,"
I say. "Yes," she says, the woman
who lost her shape and good looks
but still likes men so I see her hanging
around with deadbeats, settling for what
she can get, "red shoes, but none
of them fit. Tall heels, pumps, pointed toes . . ."
I heard someone died in her apartment
and the ambulance rolled off with the body.
Tenants bitched, but at least
he didn't fume up an unrented room—
like that guy who put a needle in his arm,
curled into his own lap and proceeded
to smell like trash, cheap
lunch meat going bad. "Round toes . . ."
sighs the woman as she steps out, turns
down the hall where low wattage
has started to flinch, and I am left
thinking of red shoes, snake skin,
suede, buckled or sleek, strappy
or tied. This is my floor, but how
did I get here? Not on girly shoes with heels
that step at a clip, or with the smart tap
of the no-nonsense shoe that means
business, or the deadly stiletto whose toe

targets the lit
end of a tossed cigarette. None of them fit.
Only the color fits, color of damage, bad
luck and bad calls—makes me think
of that street chick who flipped out, sobbed,
rubbed her bloody face against the paint job
in the hall, like a pirate signing her name
with a X. That signature sticks to the wall, hangs
in the air—a pulp red smear gone dry, shade
of some Italian leather we won't get to wear.

LAST LIST: TENEMENT LEXICON

I

What I Am Called

Miss Lady
Boss Lady
Homegirl

Girl
     Red
Babe Doll
Mary (?)

The Writer
Tough Little White Girl

Amiga
Chica
Darlin'

La Roja Loca

II

What I Should Be Called

Our Lady of Financial Sorrows

Our Lady of Beneficent Talent

She Who Should Be Paid Attention To

Miss Galaxy   Miss Netherworld
Miss Parking Space

Astarte   Leaping Deer
Philip Marlowe

Late-Night Sue
A Relatively Sober Dorothy Parker for the New
Millennium

Frank O'Hara in a
                    Joan Didion Mood

La Mujer Bellisima
Amiga
My Friend

My Love

SONG OF THE ICONOCLAST

These two stop me at the corner:
"Are you saved?"
"Oh what does that mean,"
I say, "saved?"

And whose capital are you,
whose savings?

Bills—
pressed smooth, kissed,
and laid in a long envelope,
they sleep between mattress
and box springs, "Saved,"
as the old lady puts it,
"for a rainy day."

Gold coins—
the pirate bites them to see
if they're real, then heads
towards Shoptown
with the highwayman,
bandit, gunsel, and parolee.

But no one holds me in the bank
to money-up interest. No one
blows me at the track.
I bet all I'm worth on myself,
then go off at a gallop.

You God who saves,
you Devil who spends,
try and catch me.

7.3

It's as if my room's been depressurized, the bravado
sucked out. See what a sudden loss of confidence can do?

The environs rattle their cage, bring on
an attack of nerves like nothing I've known since

the Fun House at Ocean Beach—those jet bursts
of air, the mechanical lady shrieking like an inmate.

But I don't have time to review this life flashing
past my eyes like the preview of a low budget movie,

there's death to work on.
Who has copies of my unpublished works?

If my cats crawl out of the wreck, how will they live?
Does this mean I'm off the hook for those parking tickets

and credit card debts? Like a fool I follow
everyone's advice, leap for the doorframe,

which will snap like breadsticks when the floor
caves, the ultimate letdown.

When it stops my sense of The Real won't quit
shaking. Bad

Earth. The blue-dark mother holds us and her love
turns.

A.M./P.M.

I A.M.

It's easy: open your eyes then lie
as if clubbed by some outmoded weapon,
a blackjack.
Your body feels huge like a bloodhound's.
Why get up? You've done it—
mailed hundreds of letters, met over lunches,
driven every freeway west of Vegas,
north of Escondido.
You've had fevers, brainstorms, silly affairs.
No wonder you can't rise, stoned like this—
pebbled—by your dinky past.
And then there's that future back-firing
into each day, and bucking your plans.
It's best to stay put, sleep. Consider:
they say if one inch of those weighty, packed-
hard stars, Black Holes, landed on Earth
it would fall through the world. You bet
it would still not fall so far as you.

II P.M.

Now your fretful body starts getting ideas.
Rush out and invent a new misdemeanor!
Collect names from restroom walls
then call everyone for a good time!
Of course you can't sleep—you've shrunk.
You're pinballs propelled through a course
where everything's flashing.

With one blanket you're hot, with none
you're cold. Now you're too big again!
You toss and turn like the throes of history.
You shouldn't lie here, anyway, stupid
like this, when you have errands to run—missions!
You should rush out and found a better religion,
or locate the thumbprint that will nail the killer,
or burst into a burning two-bedroom rental
and emerge with the toddler and her
Sear's photo portrait. How can you sleep?!
Out there, people pour down boulevards, famished,
love-drunk, their animal genius leaving swathes
of atomized light. But you?
You are that creature your life is wasted on,
the one who thrashes angrily all night
on the mattress, frightening the cats.

"I DON'T LIKE COFFEE—
IT MAKES ME THINK OF DEATH"

I FIRST CUP

                         Yes
but only if you gaze down
as into the far still
mouth of a
well where a tossed
                         coin
never stops
turning
            heads
                     tails
heads   and the clasped
dark leans
against the gypsy
lines of your palms
and the result of
the toss   your fortune   your
life   that Wish-in-
Nose-Dive is far
gone still
   falling

II SECOND CUP

                       Yes
but only if you gaze
down through your own

hands cupped like a
beggar's with a circle
of dark at the center like
the pipeline or porthole
keyhole
to a shadow world
because you've stayed up
all night on nothing
but blues and black
coffee and the sound
of windy traffic
outside your door
which reminds you
of death or is that
the coffee?

To be safe pour your
self another *bottomless cup*
as they used to say in
the diners and don't

                    sleep.

664-8630

For Ted Schmitt (1940 – 1990) and many others

I pass this number
in my phone book, the seven everyday
digits a sequence I won't dial
anymore—

like passing a house abandoned but
filled with echoing
rooms that were lived in. Till
now.

If I called I would hear
. . . what? A buzzing like a station
shut down for the night,
the TV screen filled with
snow?

Or has the phone line snapped
overhead, the late messages
heading for a long
fall?

No good asking like a child
why do people die? I
call

but in a room where a man's
things have been folded and packed
as if to follow him on the next train
after

a phone rings,
rings, and there is no
answer.

DEAR HOMEBOY

Something kinda stealthy loiters
near my door but it's not
you—just air turned grainy
violet where night and city
meet. Know what's going down?
Total eclipse of the moon,
Kid. It's pretty dim
out. The gas station's block
of light—like the landmark
at the world's end—says
jump off here.
If you were there you'd use it
to check out your reflection
on the hood of someone's car.
You'd use the neighbor's zinnias
to wipe the street life off your feet,
use your condition as an alibi:
It couldn't 've been me, man,
I'm, like, dead!
You'd consider knocking, take on
that shrewd look you always got
to hide a mind just half
made up, one hand idly questioning
the spot around your ribs where
blood streaked out on asphalt
and turned black, *looked*
black, in the liquor store blur
and bulb of ambulance. Look
up: a tablet dissolving
in blue mist, or mauve. I could swear

someone sauntered to my door.
The moon's half gone—I know
the feeling, sure. And you,
you're gone more.

MISSES JENSEN, APARTMENT 101

Herberto, that Herberto, what he's done now!
Little Dorothy, poor little feller's
gotten so fat—you know that stray
you named and it's left to me to feed it—
he can hardly make it over the wall, get
down here where dinner's all set out for him.
He stands up there, holds his breath,
then comes down hard like a pot
of stew meat. Poor little feller.
He gobbles up the Friskies, swallows
a half bowl of water then can hardly
get his poor heavy self back over.
So I set out that blue vinyl chair
I picked up from Woolworths,
maybe nineteen ninety-nine on sale,
down from twenty-four,
so he can aim for that, then jump
a little on it, haul himself back
over, be on his way.
But that Herberto, just because it
looks untidy—he thinks!—for the tenants,
he keeps setting it over by that beat-up tree,
moving it from where I only just
this second got finished moving it to!
What's more he keeps dumping
out the food I set down in
my little cat dishes and putting
them off to the side there.
Just because some folks on their way
to the trash can't watch where

they're going, step into the chicken-tuna
and go cry-babying down the hall,
he dumps out my cat food dishes
and puts them away. Nerve!
And next morning, Dorothy,
little Dorothy Parker, poor feller, funny
name for a boy cat, standing on
the wall outside too fat to come down
just moaning his heart out.
And my good chair on sale,
my little cat dishes white and blue
going back and forth, 'round and 'round.
Herberto, oh, oh! that Herberto!
Seems like every right thing I try
to put down in this world he sets it back!

ABOUT MISSES IVERSON

She don't open the door,
that old lady there, four-oh-six.
You know she shy, quiet, and never
do nothing, never call attention.
But the manager come for rent and she
don't open. And he, you know,
's calling *Misses Iverson!*—Come
back the next day—Heriberto—she
don't open. And he's *Misses Iverson,
you O.K.?* So he get the key.
Chained from the inside. So now
everybody wondering. Wondering.
So he come back, cut the chain lock, and
she there, eyes open, looking around,
but dying in that old bed. I guess. 'Cause
she rode out on a stretcher and never
come back. Been in that place as long
as anybody can remember but
somebody else now in four oh six. The way
I see it, she was awake enough then, she
heard, all that everybody calling her name.
The way I see it, she work for some boss,
you know, some little place, her whole
life, where they do your taxes or sell
you insurance, something like that,
and she shy and she never do nothing. Well—
she do what she supposed to do.
Now she dying she push back some—
she don't have to answer to nobody.

Don't have to jump up for every knock.
Ahh *no,* she think, *Uh Uhh.*
I ain't gonna open the god damn door!

MAN'S SHIRTS FLUNG FROM WINDOW

would make a great headline,
wouldn't it, but it's just news to me:
twisting arms and heaps of bright colors
still on their hangers.
Here's the terrible backside of the building,
overgrown, defiled by lost cats, route
to the dumpster. But now—gold flecks
on black, gold pencil stripes, like paradise
threw out some fancy stuff, used but good,
and not synthetic, silk! Well, half and half.
I call for Herberto to come fix this, too,
like he does everything—our blown sockets,
burnt wires, crumbled plaster, leaks.
If he only had the tools, right ones,
he'd repair our lives, but no one's got
that kind. *Mira*! *Camisas*! One shirt hugs
the garbage lid—an embrace tossed out
with table scraps, smashed cans.
Herberto's seen it all before. He points
to the window at the top, "There, Four-O
-Four, he's, you know . . ." His fingers curl
and he pretends he's tipping a beer,
"and she doesn't like." Guy must have
dropped a lot of cash to step into
The Dubra Room like that, pause
so the girls could check him out—
must've looked good even in bad light.
Then I recall that beefy man who knocked
at 2 a.m., asked me for three bucks.
I shut the door. Oh well, gold-on-white

hurdled on its hanger then hooked
a branch. Heaven didn't reach us.
It got snagged. I head back to my place.
Herberto climbs the stairs,
knocks. I hear her yelling through the door,
won't open up, won't take them back, rejects
it all, denies, denies. They never held her
in their arms. She never knew those shirts!

BLACK DRESS

It's *Dia de Los Muertos* all day
here in this warp and
weep of beads, story
that draws towards
an ending. This stand up shadow
would look great alongside
some skeleton's bones
in the closet, or in the arms
of a *calaca* of paper and clay.
Come, let's strip down to basics
and dance with that other self.
Baby, it's a mood piece
and Greek to me—Omega-
ville and *wine dark sea*, charred
pearl, these folds and unfoldings,
sea stored in a lady's chamber.
And oh all night it's Night
of the Hunter and Hunted For,
shady subtext, un-
transparency, flipside of that
side you face out to the world.

WHITE DRESS

Even then I knew what I didn't want: all this.
The tiny pair in formal dress set stiffly
on the cake gazed toward some outcome which
smoothed their faces blank. The creamy shapes
below them sank like sleep. They seemed
like incidentals in some melting grand design.

I couldn't melt—I poofed. My pink dress
scooped out around my knees, I couldn't press
it flat. On the stack, I saw my parents' gift,
a hand-carved birdhouse painted white
and blue. But the boring Merton's brought
a set of steak knives looking out
the window of a box, through cellophane.
(My parents were a married couple, too,
but not commonplace like that). I knew
how marriage worked, the real ones,
I'd seen T.V. I didn't want it, a house
with someone always in (except when
he was out) taking his place at the head
of the table, or retreating behind the news
in some large, commodious chair.

The bride made her rounds as if awake
inside a dream, then leaned—half
swooned—towards me. Her veil
swept around me like a mist, or net
that spilled the sudden gift of sight. I caught
her gardenia scent. I glimpsed the silk
along her neck brushed with tiny pearls, seeds

about to hatch. A burst
of dandelions would make the air fly white.
The wine I'd sipped made me feel faint,
lathed by pearl, the rush of dry
fine lace—as if man and woman, now
and ever, had fallen on me from the sky,
consummate, personal and lush.

"Darling, you look lovely!" said the face,
then seemed to drift like dawn.
The mystery of union let me go,
tossed me back into what I was before.
She seemed to float away. I seemed
to tumble on.

MARILYN IN THE LOS ANGELES CENTRAL LIBRARY

Marilyn in Art

Marilyn Among Friends

Marilyn Monroe and the Camera

Marilyn Mon Amour, the Private Album

Diary of a Love of Marilyn Monroe

Norma Jean: My Secret Life with Marilyn Monroe

Cuarenta Dias Con Marilyn

Marilyn and Me, Sisters, Rivals, Friends

Joe and Marilyn, A Memory of Love

Marilyn's Daughter: A Novel

Marilyn Monroe Confidential: Intimate, Personal Account

Marilyn Monroe an Appreciation

The Secret Happiness of Marilyn Monroe

Marilyn, The Tragic Venus

Unabridged Marilyn, Her Life from A to Z

Marilyn, An Untold Story

Diosa, Las Vidas Secretas de Marilyn Monroe

Marilyn Scandal, Her True Life Revealed

Marilyn, The Last Months

Marilyn, The Last Take

Last Sitting

Who Killed Marilyn Monroe?

Marilyn Monroe, Murder Cover-Up

Requiem for Marilyn

Sayonara, Marilyn Monroe

Legend: The Life and Death of Marilyn Monroe

Marilyn Monroe, *Que Estas en el Cielo*

The Return of Marilyn Monroe

Of Women and Their Elegance

Marilyn Monroe a Never-Ending Dream

Marilyn Monroe

Marilyn Monroe

Marilyn

HOT PURSUIT CONTINUED

So none of us up late this winter
night balmy as June can go. The motorist
jumped out and split. We ask and ask
he caught yet? —while choppers aim
their spots at angry corners where a guy
could hide. With this running man
gaining on us from the inside, this heap
boiling like big game brought down
in one shot, who can sleep?
When we do we dream up a metaphor
for life: one long skid, crash, then
flight down unlit streets. Next day,
the wreck's cleaned up, truck, tipped
traffic light, gone in nothing flat—
just the gleam of windshield underfoot.
The shapes the city makes it swallows
back, sort of like the sea. But every
block's the scene of some fool's
last ditch run for cover. Yeah—
                    we know that.

II
BROKEN AND IN NEED OF REPAIR

WAYS TO MAKE MONEY #1

We will wash your cat, your budgie,
your small, untidy, unlicensed, tree-
dwelling beast from Tanzania. We will walk
your spaniel, your grandma, smooth
the specks from her spectacles,
prop her against a sturdy surface like
a liquor store, let her stare at the view.
We will write some poems for you, for
your birthday, which everyone forgets—
not us. Or, we will write
your poems. We can make them rhyme.
Look. *From sea to shining sea*
and
from the shores of Tripoli. Or—pay
us in advance, for when your time comes.
Let A Po-et Write Your Ob-it!
We will fix your broken stuff—we
own glue. We will guard your guard dog.
We will wash your car.
We will remove from your windshield
the cheap business cards, Bible quotes,
news of parts store openings, little cries
for help cast on the waters, all the slips
of rained-on, fading paper, including
this one.

RENT YOUR INDY MOM
or WAYS TO MAKE MONEY #2

I

Sad Boy! You never had the mom you wanted. Rent our 1960s Counterculture Mom. She'll stich and knit and macramé your clothes, and chew leather till it's soft to shape sandals for your precious feet. You'll catch your first Brain Swamp concert (just before they switch from light to heavy metal) at twelve days old. She'll need no man but you. She'll rock you in her arms along with everything she swears—she knows—is true: that you'll grow to be a successful, happy man, the sky will shower blessings shaped like tiny birthday cake rosettes, and soon—no more war.

II

Sad and Cheated Boy! Your mom wasn't what you'd hoped for. Rent our Traditional 1950s Mom and Apple Pie. Oh the delight of peeling back thin foil to reveal three white slices—protein floating in its tray of pale gravy—then the patch of yellow kernels, then boiled, sugared apples with some dough. And, yes, the miracle of TV's on, an old man delivering the news, then *Cowboys*! And tomorrow, a trip downtown! She'll take your tiny hand in hers and drag you, red and howling, away from department store displays filled with every gleaming, candy-colored thing you ever wanted and still can't have.

Broken Rules #1

A WOMAN WITH A CHAMELEON ON HER HAT

"Never write a poem about a woman with a chameleon on her hat."

Why does she wear a chameleon
and why there? Why here?
Everyone is talking but her.
The women put their heads together
and speculate: *Is that her true color?*
Her hands are gloved, so we can't see them.
Carefully she unfolds a small
square of paper and reads it.
She nurses her drink.
She guards her secrets.
She is keeping her options open.

Everyone is drunk at this party.
It has been a hard year.
The chameleon is sleeping it off.
From across the room
a stranger has fallen in love.
He keeps thinking *gray-eyed Athena*,
for some reason, and can't stop.
If he told her of his love
the chameleon would wake, round
the brim of her hat, alert,
half dangerous, a new color.

Everyone has come to this party.
The world came, even the poor

dressed up. But who invited that woman?
She's from the outside, now
there's a strangeness among us.
And that thing is a lizard.
Sometimes it stands up pointing
its face, such a tense, immediate
presence, a contrast to everything.
Sometimes it lies low. Sometimes
it may not be there at all.

What does she observe that we don't?
The nearest fire exit—on planes,
the escape hatch to get out.
Does she know the whereabouts
of the unchartered fault lines?
No, no one knows.
She lights a cigarette and smokes
as if this were the 40s.
She dresses against fashion.
She never wears furs, she prefers
something living.

Her hat brim shadows her eyes.
When she tips back her head
they come out from under.
Her eyes are clear but you can't read them.
Why wear a chameleon?
Because everything is more than one color.
Because our lives keep changing
and we can't stop.

Broken Rules #2

EVERYWHERE I GO THERE I AM

"No self-pitying poems."

Two women lean at the cafeteria
counter in the last great
dime store downtown, Broadway

off Sixth. They've journeyed
through aisles of shower caps,
dollar jewelry, baby toys,

just to sit down. The old one's
hair's gone pale, tied back
like a trickle of snow,

her limbs so thin she could be
lifted on strings
like a puppet, then let go.

But her friend had looks—she maybe
followed her star, came West.
Now she nightshifts someplace

for her bus fare and low rent.
She thinks, I bet, *to hell with it*
and rubs out her cigarette. *Some star.*

Yeah, it all adds up to one long
ride down
the escalator to the bins

of cheap stuff where you settle
for what you can get, then back up
for some lukewarm tea.

Don't be fooled, it's just
another half-disguised
poem about me.

Check back in twenty years
or so, you'll see.

STREET DUMB

Between the firehouse and hospital
my place—eleven seven five—
hangs above the mini-mart. All night
sirens bleet *someone's left alive*
or *someone's not quite killed.* Red
lights, whirly-gig and thrilled,
freezy hot, feed their urgencies
to the dark. But blood
on asphalt under streetlight
isn't red, it's almost black—
like someone smudged
the guy's cut-out silhouette.
No, that's a lie—scrap that.
Shadow exited a rip
so small I couldn't put it back.
No, oil thinned by shadow
drizzled from a tank.
No. I saw a man die but didn't get
shook up. I just went stupid. Blank.
So even when they said, "Well
he won't have to pay his rent,"
pulled the sheet across his face,
closed it—a long
letter no one sent—I was *huuh?*
like *duh!* like I didn't even know
what that meant.

THE DIVORCING MAN

His wife is this heart-shaped
metallic balloon that got loose
and bobbed up high over
the jammed intersection where
he sits at his wheel, with a front
and back seat, a bumper
at either end, and another
before and behind him.
The heart glints
like a second prize, dangles
a string for holding, except who
has arms that long anymore?

Broken Rules #3

HURRYING TOWARD THE PRESENT

"No past tense permitted."

—Kay Boyle, *A Poem for Samuel Beckett*

Darlings, this may be the only
great escape we ever make:
start dropping your past
behind you—seeds, kernels
to be pecked up by scavengers.
You won't find your way back.

Or try this: package it,
mark it *Was*. Leave it in a locker
at the Greyhound Bus station.
Leave the door ajar. Let
a thief inherit it. You can bet
it'll dog him like it dogged you.

Step smack-flat into
the blasting present,
your heart asserting *Now-Now*.
You feel neither the pain
left behind, nor what waits
tapping its hard foot
up ahead.

And now, stand up the future!
Let it go on pacing and cursing
as it peers towards your whereabouts,

and the cat's eye gleam
of its watch calculates
the lateness of the hour.

EURYDICE FINALLY FINDS
A WORKING PHONE BOOTH

"Meanwhile, work boats from two private companies arrived to gently vacuum dead fish from the rocky floor of King Harbor marina, where 30 to 40 tons of sardines remained submerged . . ."

"About 50 tons of hot dog-sized fish have been scooped from the water . . ."

—Regarding massive sardine die-off, *Los Angeles Times*, 3/10/2011

I've got bad news
and worse news: first, I'm in hell
and, secondly, I'm calling collect. Come get me.
And hurry up, will you, I don't like the weather—
muggy most days. And this seaside town
that maybe served once as an annex to heaven,
is shot, well, to hell I guess, the wharf eaten,
strewn with threadbare nets, stalls
where fishermen displayed the open-eyed shine
of the day's catch just rotted sticks now,
the storefronts turning to salt then
to thick and itchy air. Wow—
what was that? Can you believe all those words
jumped from my mouth? Don't know
how I did it, but it seems as much poetry leaps
up from hell as wafts down from heaven.
Anyway, I'm running out of coins,
and their metal rubs my thumbs green. Weird.
It's the atmosphere—no fun to breathe but we get
these killer sunsets. The discharge of tail pipes
and smoke stacks makes them pretty. See,
all the junk you guys put out finds its way

down here. Our waves exude a bluish
iron gleam, and there's no cute fishes left—
just toothy things retro-fitted for the fight ahead.
Get it? Hell as preview of the future earth.
Don't worry, Babe. Roll your fat bus down
every dirt road and four-lane boulevard—
the vibe of cylinders, that's your music now.
Just kidding! Get me outta here! And this time,
Orp, we'll make it. Because at this dump,
believe me, you will not look back.
Oh, but one good thing—no flames here,
no brimstone, like the Fundamentalists believe.
Although when I wade thigh deep
in that infected, oil-glossy tide, it kinda burns.

MEDUSA DEPRESSED

Tell me about it, for me
everyday's a bad hair day.
And no stylist in town'll
give me the latest non-
peroxide tint—they make
excuses, "Uh, sorry,
Ms. Medusa, we're all
booked up, no way."
Then people blame me
for my looks—jerks!
And shampoo? Yeah, *right*.
When soap gets in their eyes
try to pull a comb through *these*—
vipers you know, all of them
pissed off at each other and
the world. So, sure, they bite.
Plus: Girlfriend, you think
you've got it rough finding
men who aren't just mush?
All mine are rock!
But could I chip through
the granite and pull the men
back out? Guess not.
All I want 's a guy
who'd putter around out back,
fix things, come in handy.
And I'm still a babe—get past
my head, I'm hot.
I'm snake-bite candy.
In my dreams I let down, down,

my silky teen-queen locks,
and some cute prince climbs up.
If he asked I'd tell him, Oh,
those sculptures all along the walk?
Tributes to men who loved me
at first sight—that dangerous
emotion, like crystal Meth. *Whoosh!*
Dude,
      I took their breath.

THE PERFECT MAN
(A NURSERY STORY)

For the men who've asked me,
Why isn't there a perfect man
in any of your plays?

                 He's lonely.
There is only one of him.
He's like the last-of-its-kind
someone captured
and shipped back to the zoo.
                 Except he
has never been captured, only
by the mirror that captures
his image, speaks
the same reassurance:
you are the fairest . . .
He sighs and straightens his tie.
It's terrible being a myth.
Why can't he do goofy
ordinary things—
cruise down boulevards,
be in a play?
                 He moves
through his rooms,
which are clean
as deep space and stuffed
with pure light.
Why can't he be bad?
He fires a cigarette, lets it droop
from his lips with a roguish

nonchalance. No ash
falls from its tip.
                    No smoke rises.

Broken Rules #4

ANSWERS AND FOUR COMMON QUESTIONS

"Never end a poem on a question—it feels so incomplete."

I

Against Oxygen, against Nitrogen,
its wavelengths break then scatter
their trick shots of light, fooling
the eye, and the mind's eye, so
we can believe there's a ceiling,
a cushioning softness, we might fall up
into, and somewhere an end to all this.

Why is the sky blue?

II

If the weather is right, if the omens
are good, if I can pencil it in, subtract it
from my tax bill, if my mother says yes, if
my ex-wife says no, if I have money
in the bank, time on my hands, a bounce
in my step, and a rose in my white lapel.
If your body will never grow old,
if you can restore my youth, interpret
my dreams, deliver me from evil, save me
from my creditors, then yes, then yes,
then oh yes . . .

Do you think we should get married?

III

a) Irreconcilable differences.

b) She was full.
  or
    She was fulfilled
      or
    She was fed up.

c) She knew the discussion would go on
   without her, and on, like a tree falling
   and falling while she was not there to hear.

Why did she leave the table?

IV

Moment upon moment more life like
this, which feels still incomplete, is never
enough, so that even when happy we imagine
some greater happiness, one with the intensity
of dreams, available in some other realm not
here, where we push our bodies greedily
into the future, our hands outstretched,
clamoring, asking, asking,
What's next? What's next? What's next?

MORNING AFTER THE 6.1

At work we tell
and tell of disasters, the wrack
of flood tides, wind chill, uncontained
fires, eye of storm, core of volcano.
And remember the Silmar when
the ground pitched like the deck of a ship?
Power lines jerked and snapped.
Electricity bolted into the dark
like unspeakable language.
We're too happy to work. Survival
has gone to our heads like pirate rum.
Dead, stand back and make way.
Here come the living.

SHORT POEM DEMANDING
MASSIVE SOCIAL ACTION

I wake up—my cold is gone. Already
my cats are darting about with polite
expressions on their faces, pursuing
their indeterminate plans.
The wine glasses from last night's party
rise from here, there, a sort
of shimmering in the room
like the presence of imagination.
Someone built these castles in the air
then couldn't break the spell.
Something hums with desire and possibility.
People, why keep blaming the world
when the world is this full?
Fling open your windows,
throw out the old way of thinking.

Performance Poem Series*:*
Warning—Does Not Work on Page! #1

LOVE POEM WITH NO WHIMPERING

When I met you I was hooked,
disarmed, altogether dumbfounded.
I was discomfited!
 An effect was being had on me.
I was had, I was taken in—
taken for a ride. I'm still riding—
who could get off; it's too fast to jump
and, anyway, I'm handicapped by all this emotion.
I'm not used to this—I used to be normal.
Oh people put down *Normal* but
just wait till it's gone.
Don't look at me—my savoir-faire's all messed up.
This is your fault—you should be arrested,
you Felon and Purveyor of Misdemeanors!
Look, now my lines are ragged and this poem looks ugly!
This is your fault you *Miscreant*. Well it's not mine is it—
did I call an 800 number and order *Big Trouble?*
Did I send in a three-by-five card and subscribe to *Emotion?!*
You make me write sloppy, galloping, pitch
forward poems no one will publish!
You make me leave out all the details . . .
except I think I remember your hair.
You make sex come off almost
as good as it looks in the movies.
You make me happy sometimes—
but let's not get sentimental, and anyway
you don't all that often!

You ask me for a love poem,
remember? You get this like a fastball.
Any man, any man like *you*,
asks Lummis for a love poem,
he'd better stand back.

Performance Poem Series*:*
Warning—Does Not Work on Page! #2

ASPIRE TO BE LESS STUPID
or
SHOOT ME BEFORE I POST AGAIN

A thin cloud cover cools the moon.
I have eaten four small dumplings
of chocolate. It is ten o'clock, p.m.
To Terry who calls Obama a Muslim,
a Marxist, a Communist, and what's
worse, a Socialist, and a Kenyan, and
what's worse, a Foreigner, who writes,
"all the moves this guy makes are not
in line with a free Democratic society,"
and "we're about to be taken over
without a fight. People wake up!"
this is my last post:
Many thanks for the helping of preposterous
accusations, refried urban legends, program-
matic clichés, and—to top it off—colorful
paranoia sprinkles.

A few sidewalk-sprung palms draw
their lean lines against
the backdrop of sky, violet, grayish,
mauve. I am brewing caffeine.
It is 11:09 p.m.
To Peck who wrote, "Let's see,
she is fat, she is ugly and she is black.
What else is there to know?"

This is my last post:
One) For all those calling Oprah "fat":
Please give us your height and weight.
Two) For those calling her "ugly":
Please post your photo.
Three) For those calling her "worthless"
or "a fake": Please name what you have done
for your family, your community, and the world.
Four) For those writing "Who Cares?"
Explain what vague itch or irritation
stirred you to release a filament of your listless
self out into the world wide web.
Five) For all those posting other stupid,
vicious remarks, answer this question.
Jealous?

The grass caught in the streetlamp light
reveals intimations of rain. Coffee's cold
now but I'm into my third cup. On my screen,
the note in the corner says 1:22 AM.
To James who wrote "Barrack go
Back to your afracan country, you
are a discrase to the united states
of america.join your mexican leader,
you are so stupid you did not
stand up for the U.S. then you
invited this idiot for dinner and we
the taxpayers paid for it"
This is my last post:
Wow, James, let's see: you can't spell
the name of the president (but nice
to know if you ever post on the topic

of an Army barrack *you'll manage O.K.)*
you misspell a whole continent.
You spell "disgrace" D-I-S-C-R-A-C-E
(no surprise you can't manage the root
of that word, "grace"), you can't
 punctuate, you know nothing
about international affairs, or domestic
affairs, and you can't think. So, gee, I guess
we should all follow your lead from now on.

I've reformed—I have given up coffee.
Gallo's Vermouth gives off the fragrance
of spices. Now that curvy moon's
under water, under a spell. Oh,
out of the rain that curvy moon doesn't
have sense to come in. It's 2:39 A.M.
To Zipp,
This is my last post
You are a bozo and should stop
announcing your rash, unreasoned, foolish
and bazaar comments in a public forum.
Obama resign? Ridiculous! But, oh,
of course, anyone you didn't vote for
should resign. And everyone who—in a spec-
tacular show of will power, political savvy
and negotiation succeeds in getting bills
through Congress, bills you don't agree with,
should resign. Thank goodness you're not
in charge. There wouldn't be any America
haters because there'd be no America left
to love or hate. We'd have a monarchy, with
a really crummy, jackass king!

Never mind what the moon's up to now.
It's 3:07. No Vermouth left in this glass
bottle. To Booti who wrote,
"Let the socialist Marxist Libtards
go out and wash all the oil off the fish
and birds, ha, ha, ha,"

This is my last post
Booti, Itty-Bitty, Why did you turn out so badly,
such a failed human, such a blob, why so angry
and friendless—was it your parents,
your upbringing? Did they dump you off
at the TV screen, to be raised by old videos
of "Porky's II" and "I Spit On Your Grave?"
Or, were you kidnapped by Gypsies,
left in a forest then adopted
by hyenas who'd escaped from the zoo? No—
couldn't be that, because then at least
you'd be interesting!
Maybe you just popped out this way,
an ignorant, crude baby determined
to get worse. Oh there's no hope, no hope
for you, except—this: read books, books of quality,
with words like "radiant," "disorder,"
"Babylonian" and "Cinnamon Buffet."
Read the true news or, at least, news
that's closing in on the truth, watch smart TV—
it exists! Aspire to be less stupid.

It's 3 A.M., long time the rain fell, fell and
went on falling. Still it falls . , , Duh
What else *would* it do? Rise? Salt

would be good. Chips. Salt.
James is back! "Why didn't you post
my comment Yahoo? You at Yahoo
don't like what I say? You deny me
my first amendment right to freedom
of speech/expression/the press?
Well screw you Yahoo!"
This is my last post.
Dear Yahoo, Thank you for your public service
in sparing us the moronic ranting of this simpleton.

It is later than 4 A.M., and still The Great Dumbness,
force-fed and force-feeding, bubbles and swells,
fattens, somewhere in the land, across
the purple mountain majesties and on
the fruited plain. And who can stave it off,
beat it back, who but I? And how, ever,
can I sleep? **This is my last post . . .**

DEALS KEEP FALLING THROUGH

O.K., who dealt this hand of raw deals?
Our hearts may be broken but
they still work super late. *Tick tock
tick* . . . That's time wasting—byte
by byte—on wheels. We ride
past corner malls that weren't
there last week while all
around us the slow-
motion show glows white—the mute
drift down and burn
of dreams unspun like movie reels.
Step over the Styrofoam cup
smashed flat, a bottle of Thunderbird
sucked dry, a windshield's
safety glass, shattered and safe
for nothing, right? This is Hollywood.
This is the backlot of our discontent
we gripe—our shows
picked up then cancelled, or just
dispersed into the night. Why try?
Here is the fallen deal
that wears our face. For once,
let's not to our own selves
lie. Admit
           that it fits just right.

Broken Rules #5

SOUL FILLET
or
HOW TO WRITE THE LOVE POEM

"Never use the word 'soul' in a poem."

I

Then call it *Atva*, like the Hindus—why
not? Let it move up and down the wheel
of reincarnation—now tiger, now trumpet-
shaped flower, now peddler of almonds
and figs. *Samsara,* the name of this falling
and rising.

Don't say My soul longs for you,
say, In this life I am occasioning a body
that needs yours. And wants.

No, don't name anything. Say,
It's yours, take it—still red
from the hunt, brushed with pollen,
and ripe
with that unexpungeable scent
of the human it spreads over the world.

II

Don't say, I love you with my whole soul,
love with your *sole.*
Because it's born like other fish,

but in some slow dissolve, over hours,
days, through a body more liquid
than flesh, the left eye slides
towards the right. On the ocean floor
it lies down on its eyeless side.
It can do little but see
and wait for those shellfish
the fishermen call "crusty stars."

From the cracked, chewed bottom
of things, it endures—a steady gaze
towards the surface,
                              and the surface world.

III

Reader, Stranger, take these leftover bits,
the findings I couldn't fit in:
the lemon sole with its smooth

skin pattered like marble, the sand dab,
smear dab (*smear dab!*) and that flatfish
named the sweet fluke.

Imagine—*sweet fluke!*

Take this from the Sufi scriptures,
from that one who created all things:

"I was a hidden treasure,
and I desired to be known."

THE NOT SONNETS

I Blood

I never liked onions, the one time
I cut them it's for you and straight
off the knife goes for the bone.
It's as if I've struck gold, oil,
a nerve. My hand
fills with such heart-felt color.
I can no longer read
the future on this palm, but here
is a valentine that won't quit, ink
to write a thousand poems
no one will read
or letter that comes back
No Such Resident.

II Smoke

I remember everything: the precise
outlook of the stars, at a nearby
table, a smoking cigarette, ticking
watch. (I lie about the watch,
the cigarette, but not the smoking,
ticking.) Love, when
I looked in your eyes I glimpsed
plundered cities, heard cries.
But that was then.
These days I tell my students
never say "I remember."
You're writing the poem, aren't you?
Of course you remember.

III Chocolate

Footprints
end at the wall—otherwise
the room is in perfect order.
Who cleaned up after himself removing
all signs of struggle? There's a mystery
at the heart of this poem I don't understand.
What, did you take me for the victim?
I'm the detective seeking a clue, the line missing
or stolen: *Line That Would Explain Everything.*
But there is only this title hinting
at darkness or sweetness, ways
to lose one's way or just
be lost.

Broken Rules #6

TO HIS SHY MISTRESS

"No dead metaphors."

Your eyes are deep pools, your cheeks
roses, your lips rubies, my love, my
"monster." The maid on seeing you dropped
the heirloom china. What commotion.
Fair Ellen, furious I hadn't chosen her,
fainted towards the arms of her second choice.
Men blanched and shrank inside
their greatcoats, became, I think,
the small men they really are.
Mistress, no wonder you are shy.
When we linger near the arboretum
near the roses, bees engage
the roses of your cheeks. Small
insects drown in those azure pools.
It's difficult for both of us; your lips
hard (though not difficult) to kiss,
like flesh turned
to marble by a peevish jilted god.
Nights I lie weeping in your arms.
You tease that if my eyes fill too,
you might drown. I say—
in such a pooling up we both
might drown. It's your mind
I love, its swift, surprising charm,
your words, more like poetry than
the rhymes that dreamed you up

piecemeal. You say —
if only I could wish my face of *things*
away and be made of shadows
like the moon.

From far off, we can hear the minor poets
bawling. "We meant cheeks *like* roses,
lips *like* jewels! . . ." —
men with gold tipped walking sticks,
watches on gold chains.

Incomparable love, take me.
What do I care what people think?

MELANCHOLY POEM SET IN 1951,
IN THE PITTSBURGH OF MY IMAGINATION—
WITH FORMAL ELEMENTS

The city's weighted with greyish heads
on sheets emitting a measly light.
All lovers lose their lovers
here in the middle of the night.
He slips through the fire exit,
takes the easy route.
Or he'll toss a cigarette that shrinks
down, down, then out—
then rise like smoke from bed.
He'll feel vaguely sorry.
Or she goes out how she came in,
and leaves a lip print hard as lead
on a glass of Gilbey's Gin—
smudge of factory red.
They let the sleeping lie
where they went down, but not in glory.
They leave a thin scent in the air
of who they were, what happened here.
No doubt it tells a kind of story,
but they let bygones go by.
They don't let the thing get old,
here, where the unloved wake up alone,
their hearts loud in the tin cup cold,
and these mementoes hiss *memento mori*.

SAD POEM IN WINTER —
WITH ASSONANCE, CONSONANCE,
AND OTHER OCCASIONAL EFFECTS

for the late Chuck Gresham, who understood

Air snaps
open the window with such
a shock that out of my sleep
I sit up. Rain jabs
where it doesn't belong.
Some fat bad wolf got in.
Fine, I'm not
too old for a thrill — blow
this straw house down.

Hell caught
chills out there battling for a stretch
of ground. And the garbage pressed
to the pavement's getting a lift —
skid marks and spit — the oils
of neighborhoods rise.
You'd think in such downpour
a city'd come clean —

I should
at least, in this water
ripped through the screen.
You'd think a night of this kind
would deliver some miraculous sign.
But there're just those nail-hard
meters of the street, red tongues
sprung up: *you're out of time.*
Oh this could get good,

like a club act, like a dream
of Hollywood. Meanwhile
the rain strikes swollen rags,
shopping carts, the essential
smashed flat Styrofoam cup.
I want to burn like a saint,
but I can't, so I'll smoke
my last menthol down to the butt

and pray
for pnemonia in this damp. Oh look.
—Girl's bought the news and under
The Times *View* tries to push home.
Some guys push in angling
for a little heat, but she's had enough
and it's wet. I should be out there
with them, with all of the washed up.

Broken Rules #7

MY WORST POEM

> *"Never write a poem that says* words fail me."

Well you don't pay my rent, don't bring
home the bacon, don't crown me Most
Celebrated Aging Poet Princess in the Land.
Words, you disappoint me.
Right now, for instance, here,
in my worst poem yet.
It's not my fault, I'm a conduit!
You guys march through me then
cue up on the page like
Depression era bread lines.
For once, why don't you do it for me
like you did it for Liz Bishop?
(Or at least can't we
twist again like we did last summer?)
And would it be too much to ask,
please, for an image?
I mean we're making this poem, see,
so produce a man on a ledge
or buttered toast on a serving tray.
Words, give me danger then
gimme something to eat.
Don't run lukewarm, lukecool,
be Cool Hand Luke.
Don't be all
Send me into the morning
and

Soon it will be dark
and
There was nothing to be found.
But none of this either:
The incandescent spectacle of singularity
Fixing nothing/That toils in
scrambled magnitudes . . .
So what I'm saying—vitality!
But I don't want some vapor-brained
open mic monologue about going
down on some jerk at a party!
Be clear. Be dark. Raise the heat.
Put an old LP on the turntable. Get me
a little bit drunk.
And muster some wit, or at least
plain proletariat humor. A joke!
Knock knock.
Who's there. **48.**
No one.
No one who?
No one/der this house looks unfamiliar, I'm on the wrong street!
But since I'm here, Stranger, may I come in for a glass of cognac
with crushed ice. I should mention my name—Nohwan Hoo,
the private eye straight out of the new Korean paperback series
and this is my story . . .
Damn, I'm digressing again!
Words, you digress!
You lead me on, thither
and dither (*dither!*) down
Primrose Lane past the statuary, past
the boy angel shouldering
a platter of grapes, and into

a La Brea Tar Pit.
Words fail me.
You fail me, Words.
I've had it with you, I'm—*snip!*—
severing our relationship.
Pack your bags. Take a hike.
Make yourself scarce. Hit
the road, Jack. Blow
town. Split the spot. Buzz
off, push off, shove off. Go fish!
Get lost. Get thee behind me,
shrimps! Get thee to a nunnery.
Scram. Beat it. No . . . wait! *Wait!*
Wait. Words . . .

forgive me.

Broken Rules #8

TOO

". . . Don't steal other people's lines."

I saw the best minds of my generation destroyed by madness,
      starving hysterical naked,
dragging themselves through the Negro streets at dawn looking
      for an angry fix *too!*

Broken Rules #9

PINK (REFUSAL TO LOOK THROUGH ROSE COLORED GLASSES)

"Never use the color pink in a poem."

I AGAINST

No primroses!
Nothing prim, only erotic
unstoppable flora with colors
that jangle like a sprung alarm,
flowers of hothouse and heatstroke,
out of control like heady gossip.
No twilight, no temperate glow!
Turn on the spotlight, floodlight, write
in the illumination of a burning house.
No babies!
No big, pale inexperienced babies!
No birthday cakes!
Celebrate with six altar candles
in the ribs of a roast sow.
Forsake bubble gum!
Chew nothing but bits of blown
tire from a vehicle
that careened off the road.
Reject Pepto Bismol! Deny pigs!
No ribbons and bows!
Anything's better—a noose
for hanging is better!
Beware hair curlers of pink foam.

They'll cushion your head from
the point of that unrestful dream.
Beware the mild rose soaps
in a gift pack—
        nothing comes clean.

II IN DEFENSE

But *Pink*—the sound
you have to make, like the clip
of purse-size sheers, precise.
The prick of *pin,* the point,
it draws a harder color
out, one drop. You see, there's *ink.*
To write. One word. Too light?
It darkens as it dries. It costs
a bit, extracts
its pinhead price, not much but
—you know—words add up.

FRAGMENT ENDING WITH 19 WORDS
FROM DELMORE SCHWARTZ

For the air some flavor, citrus
or mint, not ash, not crust,
for the tongue a brightness,
somewhere the ribboned carousel,
the arabesque, some low sweet
gondola under all this—this life—
some clear drinking spring, not
Shop, not Pay, but O My Love,
and Ever Arrival, Ever Letting
Go, newness upon newness,
and what swift one comes, or
slow, a rising to greet, sweet
thing or dark, a rising to face,
for always that soft thorn
of the self, star-like, core-lit,
shall ignite us alive—
some other world, some world
of goodness, some other life,
some life where the nobility
we admire is lived.

LAST REPORTS FROM THE GONDOLA
SUSPENDED BY BALLOONS

> "Three months ago a Japanese piano tuner
> attempted to float over the ocean in a gondola
> suspended by balloons and has not been seen since."
>
> —*The Los Angeles Times, 1993*

Laborers, tax payers, husbands
to unfulfilled wives, wives to workhorses
of middle management, you bearers
of just-bearable burdens, appointment keepers
and risers-on-time, good citizens loyal
to the Emperor, friends,
look! In all the world there's just one
Japanese piano tuner gazing down
on the Pacific from a gondola
held up by balloons. I am the last
possibility that has not been exhausted.

The climate is fine, cool sunlight up here
where my loneliness rings
like a tuning fork, and a slow stream
on the Persimmon Wind keeps me
wandering forward through the sky-colored air.
I feel like an illustration in a children's book.
Mother, when you held me wrapped
in butterfly prints did you ever dream?

Uh oh, friends, the evidence
of the gauges and my own eyes tell me
I'm starting to slip.
Could it be my plan needed fine-tuning?

This raindrop means a storm
gathers up there and down below
the sea will get even deeper.
Despite my quick adjustments
I'm losing height.
You know the feeling – like trying
to hang on to a great dream or wake
from a bad one. I wish that pane of water
were a window I'd sail through but
it's not. It's filled with sailors and still
hungry, still thirsty.

Colleagues, brothers of the guild, remind me:
in the findings of Wertheim, what
are the velocities of sound through pine,
oak, birch, through ash?
Through a *solution of common salt?*

I had a dumb and beautiful idea—
hard enough, isn't it, to stay aloft even
on a smart and homely idea.

In the sky or on earth, now just one technician
plays upon this exact terror touched by wonder.
Still, I can't help but think of a new joke—
for the Americans, it's funny
in English: that crazy tuner went up, up.
till he was lost in the high C's.

Salary men, servant women, bosses
who answer to bosses, friends, I did this

for you—you who won't recall just where or
who you were, when my decaying aircraft
became my declining boat:

Uncharted Desire,
a vibration, a question, a hung note.

THREE BLOCKS

My car takes the rain head-on like
a submarine burrowing still deeper
and up this thirstiest of streets. It's night,
so the miscellaneous lights are just
drops of milk we won't cry over,
just things we lost then found but must
leave behind again—points
of exclamations in the glossy dark.
I pass the miraculous drug stare, last
Rexall on Earth!, on Vermont and 7th—
windows covered with poster boards
urging *Hairspray, Ritz Crackers, Bic
Lighters*, the small and inconsequential.
And oh our dreams keep shrinking, smaller,
smaller . . . Now they can stand on a shelf
with the ceramic animals, now pocketsize,
now two-for-one in that bin there.
So what, I'm happy anyway in this rain.
And when I die, someday, might
as well be like that old man drowsing
now on the sidewalk, face
to the sky—people crowding around,
someone phoning for help.
So as I ride over the low river rising
on Wilshire—oh Headlight! oh Streetlamp!—
I imagine myself wrinkled with age or
too much rain, surprising the bystanders
by my resolve to lie down on the asphalt—
the voices calling *are you all right?!*
so tiny they could be the queries of mice,

or mice strangers.
The cars hitting the pools
make a hushing noise. I like
how the rain feels on my too-hot face,
and how my toes finally point
the right way: up. See?
Death is more dignified than life.
But tonight even life's not bad,
because my windshield wipers keep
flapping for take-off, my four radial tires
spin off sheets of water as they cross
6th and I'm not dead, not
yet, and oh this must be
it—Thing of Legend, Avenue
of Put-Back-Together-Again
Dreams . . .

III

THE FATE COOKIES

TAKE THAT CHANCE
YOU'VE BEEN CONSIDERING

I'm over the railing now. Down below
that gray-blue winks in the light
and wrinkles up. To me it seems
the No-Land between fact
and fiction, lies and the illusive truth.
But don't trust my take on it; I'm
in a state. *Trust me,*
says the official in so many words, after
he's inched as close as he dares without
pushing me, you know, over the edge:
Hey, what seems to be wrong?
Wow, what a leading question,
but oh I do trust him, I do. Look,
I want to say, the sky is the exact
untroubled blue of the crayon
I picked once to make the sky blue,
and the broken parts of this world
so far off that from here
there're cracks in a sidewalk. Deep down,
though I'll bet the sea's fingering the bones
of jumpers, rolling them like old ideas
that never quite took—what do you think?
But I can't, he'd conclude I was mad,
in need of emergency treatment.
The police have drawn a line the cars
can't pass. *It's a nice day,* he says,
we can talk things through. Want a hand?
I mustn't speak, just smile politely,
as if to say 'Thank you' or 'fine. You?'

From where I stand people look like ants,
that is, their hearts like the nipping
heads of red ants.
I can't explain this but suddenly
I want a bigness like the sea
or sky, a largess, an inheritance, the full
embrace. I want
to take that chance I've been considering.
Stanger, isn't it true, isn't it,
that out of every million,
nine hundred ninety-nine thousand
nine hundred ninety-nine drop
straight towards the obvious, but one
flies?

YOU'RE BROAD-MINDED
AND SOCIALLY ACTIVE

Who writes these things?
We'd say fire him but perhaps
he's supporting a family.
Please explain we want our future
to follow the ruins of the Peking duck,
not a personality profile.
And what's this lame praise?
—like something a man might say
when he's breaking it off. Listen,
you have a great mind, a beautiful soul. (Uh Oh!)
See what happens when we trust
our fortunes to others?

Still, we snap open the crisp
of sweetness with our hopes
up. Little ventricle bent by some palm,
envelope in 3-D, toss of the dice,
deliver us, send big money on the heels
of dumb luck. We draw out the slip
of news and—this is our lot?! This iota,
this tidbit of consolation!
It's enough to make us hungry again!
One of us jokes that if we eat more
we'll get really broad. (Polite laughter).
Well, we Socially Active better go
back to work and start earning
our slight rewards.

Nearby beautiful girls call
for creamy desserts, today's special
and tomorrow's. The Fates
set us on Status Quo then flutter
away from our table, to there
and there, where good luck rolls
like gold, like one ounce
investment coins from heaven.
Oh let's not go back to work, not ever!
Let's seek our true fortunes!
We shake hands like an assortment
of Musketeers and set forth.
Our dutiful bodies carry us along.
Our minds lead the way —
and the way is both broad
and great.

HELP! I'M A PRISONER
IN A CHINESE FORTUNE COOKIE FACTORY

You see this many time? Old joke.
Chinese person not write that.
I am from ancient water town of Xitang
that start in Zhou Dynasty thousand
year ago, then Tom Cruise come and run
through street for Mission Impossible
Three. Very popular.
Now I study English and work hard
at Good Luck Fortune Cookie
in City by the Bay San Francisco.
I sit where conveyor roll from oven
hot with many cookie—*cookies*—
on little plates not hard yet. *Rolls.*
Rolls from oven. I say better English.
Try. I pull cookie off fast, take little
paper from pile, put on cookie, fold
one time in hand then fold over thing.

American people want only good luck.
Chinese want good luck, they need.
Everybody same like that.
Only few do not like.
You have many more friends. Bore ING.
Young rich American boys and girls
do not like. They have only good luck
in life. Know only good luck. They read
Good fortune soon come your way now.
and roll eyes up. Bore ING.

Many times all day I take small, hot,
soft from oven, flat like pancake,
empty, no luck—no bad, no good,
no *now*, no *soon*—and put in future.
My hands take heat, my fingers
put nice words. I am not prisoner.

Many days I feel luck, *lucky.*
Today not so good. I am
Chinese Woman in Bad Mood in Fortune Cookie Factory.
Always professor writes Good Luck
fortunes and give to us, only professor.
Last night I write secret special fortunes
to make nobody feel bored and make
people not know so much what they feel now.
Now I go . . . I *am* go . . . Now I *will*
go *rogue.* See if you think.

Sometimes wise man same
as stupid man. You?

Bad luck for her who rest
too long in rest room.

Many people in two places—
not enough places.

Many people in one place make
one too many people. You?

Beware shady time, alcove and
square.

Do not be same person twice
in same river. Deep, huh?

Eye that grows on moon like white flower
knows all about it.

Sometimes free man have no fun.
Sometimes prisoner gets last laugh.

PEOPLE ARE SAYING GOOD THINGS ABOUT YOU

I

Love her fuchsia, don't you?
And her pink, so soft it's
   a face, a *look* thrown
      your way and glimpsed in a pocket
      mirror held up to the eye.
And my God that blue—
      Gem Stone . . . no, you're right,
      it's *water*, water the planes
   criss-cross, Sea of Cortez.
But, and you know where
   I'm going . . . *yes*, and how
does she do it? Where does
      she find it? Other people,
you know, have their B-
   Movie Black, So-What-Black,
      or Black-of-Deep-Thought.
But her black defeats death.
Awe. *Some.* Gotta credit her moxie—
   they said it couldn't be done.

II

When did you see her,
when last? Where? By
   moonlight or flame light
      did you see her? Did you
      see her by street lamp?
Did she head inland or
      seaward? Which ocean,
      or which stretch of desert
where men, women, have
toiled and endured?
   What did she carry? How?
Her small gold leaf volumes
   with their fine marginalia,
      a Bengalese cat
in a basket? Where can we
   find her, in what gloaming,
what dreaming, source of our
   longing, she of whom
      they say such good things?

YOU WILL VISIT A FAR-AWAY COUNTRY
THAT HAS BEEN IN YOUR THOUGHTS

By what steel capped rail—monorail—
passing through what mountain,
what tunnel, rock blasted to what
smithereens—day light on this side,
starlight on the other—may I ride
backwards into my thoughts, into
that far-away country?

DON'T OBEY THIS FORTUNE

Don't look this fortune
   in the eye. Don't look back—
eyes on the road, on the bumper
   of that van up ahead. No, don't.
Cancel that. More instructions
     to follow.
Don't eat the cookie that concealed
   this fortune—you eat it,
it's yours. Feed it
     to unparked birds. Go
wild. No, go mad
   a bit. Get the hell off the road—
Interstate 5, or whatever, straight
     as a gunshot, flat
as an open hand. Don't
   trust this direction, it's steering
you wrong. Stop and think for
     a second. Your future. Look
what you've done.
   Tsk. Eat this message. No,
burn this. No, burn.

SIMPLICITY IN STYLE WILL BRING
DESIROUS EYES YOUR WAY

Yes, the oddest dish since Salome was served John's head
as an entrée, but then foreign people have their own

ideas about food. I knew a traveler who ordered
a local delight and was presented a rice ball crowned

by Nose of Bull Moose. I might have figured
they're served somewhere unblinking and whole,

but how could I have foreseen this: me in a strange land
and Simplicity, the kitchen maid who is always in style,

entering with a side dish of eyes? I don't recall
ordering them: I'll blanch, flinch, upset my host!

But I engaged the finest chef in the region and they're not
to your liking!? I'll have him put to death, all of them—
down to the kitchen help!

Poor Simplicity trembles in the shadows.
No, I must eat them—clearly I'm some sort of spy.

Why else would I be dining with this feline,
smoke-haired man who conceals a sinister secret?

If it's not in his coat or breast pocket I must trick him
into removing his pants.

Despite my mastery of the language (I speak without hint
of accent), if I don't pick up my fork and dig in he'll know

I'm from Elsewhere. I try not to imagine what creature
viewed the world through these eyes; I lift a small slice,

place it on my tongue and hope my face reveals nothing
but the interest of a connoisseur. They are salty

like tears, of course, but if you don't look
at them looking at you they're not bad.

I sever a bit from the other with a knife that slides
sharp into stillness, and it glistens like injured sea life—

the eye, that is, not the knife, though that glistens also.
His eyes fix on mine, I mean on the ones

in my face. "Now I know you are one of us,"
he whispers, but it sounds like
                              Now you belong to me.

His eyes draw nearer like the kind that can see in the dark,
although the room is flooded with lamplight.

When he takes hold of my wrist, my hand opens with a will
of its own—which then escapes into air. A knife

drops from my palm. His smile suggests sympathy
or innuendo, classified information. Night falls.

A scrap burns between thumb and forefinger then blows
black.

Didn't I lay eyes on it once, some graph *occultus*
illustrating the collusion between sight, taste,

and desire? But what is this stealing and thief-like
weakness: poison, drugs, hypnosis? My own

treason? He tricked me; he and Simplicity are one, he
the Simple Simon who got me to taste his wares.

He draws my body from the chair and I'm annoyed
with it for going with him instead of staying with me.

There are means to deal with this situation but too
late; now I am in his arms and now his mouth passes to mine

the secret. And now it is I who have it, he who must seek
and find, take back that dark unruly knowledge

that once belonged to him. Oh I am a bad, bad
spy—I cross into enemy territory where things bear

witness, hold me in their sights. But this now I know:
those low, liquid giving parts are not the forbidden fruits,

after all, it's the eye, the desirous and tear-filled eye. It wants
everything.

A CHANGE FOR THE BETTER
WILL SOON BE MADE AGAINST YOU

Is it for me
this love you make against me?
I against the unrelenting
backdrop of this city—our minor
bungled plans against the grand one?
Will I make any sense here or
are the odds against it?
Sorry, but the cracking open
of this cookie and its fortune
got me started—reminds me
of a slender bone of poultry
grasped across a cluttered table
and what happens when two
contend for one desired wish.
You see where I'm headed?
Of course not—with all the lights
out who can tell what's what?
Sometimes to pull away
seems the same as pressing up
against you in this darkness,
like the way words and meaning
pull away or push against till
something snaps, and that cry
we don't recognize is ours.

Love,
let's lock hands and flee this jam
we're in, these consequences leaning
this way or that, and escape to the next

perilous change for the better.
See, it's fatal isn't it, this will to live?
Look what happens.

THE NIGHT LIFE IS FOR YOU

Here, on the boulevard of run-
amuck dreams, each stamped
with a doll-like face you half-
recognize as yours, the neon
displays its chilly, self-
possessed light.
But the lips on the billboards
are raspberry cream. They say
Buy me or Be me, you
can't tell. You're confused
like mad again, in this night
of mixed blessings spiked
with a ripe curse, that line
you fall for every time.
You'll drive these streets
in a trance after your death
crying I'm still here!
but now you get out and walk.
This pale, feverish presence
inside your life is you,
and those are loud strangers
gripping beers. But why die,
ever, while stores shout out
their bargains, hot CD's,
and one can gaze at the bodies
who've stopped dancing now
and stand about jaggedly
because the doorways
of rock clubs pumped them
into open air? No doubt about it,

all this is for you.
Some Doo Wop tune
on the airwave says the night's
thousand shifting eyes
are on the watch. You guess
two of them are yours.
Tonight Mr. Good
or Bad might pluck you
from the crowd.
There's some place you're
supposed to be, some fun
you're supposed to have.
It's fate, your fate, and it's open
twenty-four hours.

NOTES

The rules I attempted to break—judiciously and towards some interesting end—were contributed by the following people, most of them poet professors.

"Never write a poem about a woman with a chameleon on her hat."
   —*David St. John*

"No self-pitying poems."
   —*Carolyn Kizer*

"Never end a poem on a question; it feels so incomplete."
   —*Sylvia Rosen, a friend*

"Never use the word 'soul' in a poem."
   —*Denise Duhamel (and, by implication, Mark Strand who, many years back, included "soul" in a list of potentially damaging words he wrote on the board).*

"No dead metaphors."
   —*Donald Hall*

"Never write a poem that says *words fail me.*"
   —*Charles Harper Webb*

". . . Don't steal other people's lines."
   —*Philip Levine's full quote is "Don't cheat at cards, don't run down pedestrians, don't steal other people's lines." He asks that I include his follow-up remark: "I've stolen many lines."*

"Never use the color pink in a poem."
   —*Attributed to the late Ann Stanford*

Since the Kay Boyle quote comes directly from a published poem, I gave the full attribution under the title.

AKNOWLEDGMENTS

The Antioch Review: "Everywhere I Go There I Am"

Askew: "I Don't Like Coffee—It Makes Me Think of Death" (originally "Two Cups")

Cider Press Review: "Hurrying Toward the Present"

Eclipse: "7.3" (published under the title "Landers Quake")

The Hudson Review: "Melancholy Poem Set in Pittsburgh, 1951," "Street Dumb"

The Los Angeles Review: "Last Report from the Gondola Held Up by Balloons"

Malpais Review: "The City in My Head is Perfect" (earlier version published in *Querucs Review* under the title "Dreamt Poem")

Miramar: "Eurydice Finally Finds a Working Phone Book"

Onthebus: "A.M./P.M."

Ploughshares: "Dear Homeboy," "The Nightlife is for You"

Poetry International: "A Change for the Better Will Soon Be Made Against You," "Pink" ("Refusal to Look through Rose Colored Glasses")

Pool: "Love Poem with No Whimpering," "Don't Obey this Fortune," "You Will Visit a Far-Away Country That Has Been in Your Thoughts"

Spillway: "Ways to Make Money #1"

The Rattling Wall: "Black Dress"

The Temple and Solo: "The Perfect Man" ("A Nursery Story")

International Magazines / Newspapers

Mexico:

Luvina (U. of Guadalajara): "Man's Shirts Flung from Window"

UK:

Agenda, ("New U.S. Poets" issue): "Red Shoes," "Medusa Depressed"

The Sunday Independent: "Medusa Depressed"

Anthologies and Textbooks

Beyond the Valley of the Contemporary Poets: "Marilyn in the Los Angeles Central Library"

Blood Whispers: L.A. Poets on AIDS (Silverton): "664-8630"

Grand Passion: The Poets of Los Angeles and Beyond (Red Wind Books): "Three

Blocks," "The Woman with a Chameleon on Her Hat,"
In the Palm of Your Hand: A Poet's Portable Handbook (Tilbury House): "The
Divorcing Men"
Place as Purpose: Poetry of the Western States (Autry Museum of Western Heritage
/ Sun & Moon): "White Dress"
Western Wind: An Introduction to Poetry (McGraw Hill): "Morning After the 6.1"

Web Magazines

Connotation Press: "Hot Pursuit," "Fragment Ending with 19 Words by Delmore
Schwartz"
The Cortland Review: "Take that Chance You've Been Considering"
The Drunken Boat: "Short Poem Demanding Massive Social Action"
Ambusharts.com: "Answers and Four Common Questions"

"The Divorcing Men" was included in the chapbook *Falling Short of Heaven*
(Pennywhistle) An earlier draft of "Deals Keep Falling Through" also appeared
in *Falling Short of Heaven*